AI ISN'T ENOUGH

AI ISN'T ENOUGH

How Data and People Turn Technology
into Real Transformation

JANE DIMARTINO

Jane DiMartino
linkedin.com/in/janedimartino
jbmaiconsulting.squarespace.com

AI Isn't Enough, How Data and People Turn Technology Into Real Transformation —1st ed.

CERTIFIED

(H)

WRITTEN
BY HUMAN

DEDICATION

This book is dedicated to Gaby, Alex, and Joe.
You are my most important accomplishments.

CONTENTS

PART 4 – FUTURE-FOCUSED LEADERSHIP

ACKNOWLEDGMENTS

There are so many people and experiences that have shaped my journey, and I am deeply grateful for them. My dad, Anthony, with his entrepreneurial drive, and my mom, Connie, through her immigrant journey, taught me strength, resilience, and how far we can reach when we step outside our comfort zones. My sisters, Irene and Liz, were my first and forever confidantes—there to celebrate, debate, and support me through every twist and turn.

To my children, Gaby, Alex, and Joe—you are my daily inspiration. Your brilliance, kindness, and perspective remind me of what really matters and push me to keep learning and growing.

I am thankful for the leaders I have worked for along the way. You offered opportunities that stretched me, feedback that awakened new possibilities, and challenges that shaped my character. I also owe gratitude to my colleagues who kept me humble, opened my perspective, and made the work richer, whether in formal meetings or casual conversations outside the office.

To my mentors, thank you for believing in me when I was still learning to believe in myself. Your wisdom gave me the courage to step into roles and moments that changed the course of my career.

And a special thanks to Steve Gordon and his team at Million Dollar Author. You engaged me at just the right moment, encouraging me to take years of notes, reflections, and studies and finally bring them together in this book. Without your guidance and belief, these ideas might have stayed tucked away instead of being shared.

Finally, to the readers of this book—thank you for your time, your curiosity, and your openness. I hope these pages leave you not only with insights but with encouragement to carry your own stories forward.

AUTHOR'S NOTE

Let me start with a confession: I don't think AI is the silver bullet everyone is making it out to be. I've spent over two decades in boardrooms, on factory floors, and in coffee-fueled late-night project war rooms, and I've seen the same pattern repeat itself: shiny new technology gets all the attention, while messy data, broken processes, and human judgment quietly hold the real keys to success.

This book was born out of those moments—the ones where someone swore the new system would "fix everything," only for us to discover that half the data was missing, the workflows were more tangled than spaghetti, and the people closest to the problem hadn't been asked what they thought.

So, I didn't want to write a hype book. I wanted to write something real. Something you could read on a Sunday morning and think, *Oh, that's exactly what's happening at my company and maybe we're not crazy after all.*

What you'll find here are stories, lessons, and practical takeaways that connect the dots between data, people, and processes, without drowning you in technical jargon or expecting you to dust off your statistics textbook. Think of it as the kind of conversation you'd have on a walk. That is, ideas flow more easily, with a little back-and-forth, and space to notice connections you might otherwise miss.

And just so we're clear, I'm not here to impress you with hard skills or acronyms. Sure, I've led big transformation programs across financial services, consumer goods, tech, and beyond. I've wrestled with compliance deadlines, system migrations, and more than my fair share of Excel crashes. But those aren't the things that stick with me. What does? The sigh of relief when a team finally sees their data clearly. The spark in a room when siloed functions connect. The small wins that remind us why we bother in the first place.

Transformation, I've learned, has a lot in common with hockey. It's rarely about the highlight-reel goals; it's about the grind—the line changes, the blocked shots, the teamwork that doesn't make headlines but ultimately wins games. Big change happens the same way: shift by shift, with persistence and a team pulling in the same direction.

Outside of work, I'm happiest spending time with my grown-up children, catching a Boston Bruins or Red Sox game, or daydreaming about opening a little Greek taverna someday. The kind of place with good food, lively conversation, and maybe a bottle of wine shared among friends.

So here's my promise: this book isn't a lecture, and it's not a sales pitch. It's a collection of hard-won insights, a few cautionary tales, and maybe even a laugh or two about the very human side of data and AI. My hope is that by the end, you'll not only understand the challenges differently, but you'll see your role in shaping what comes next.

Because if there's one thing I've learned, it's this: AI isn't enough. But you might be.

INTRODUCTION

WHY DATA AS INTELLIGENCE MATTERS

The Reality of AI Today

AI is everywhere in the headlines and increasingly in the boardroom. From chipmakers that power its speed, to enterprise platforms that embed it into operations, to consumer tools like ChatGPT that millions use daily, it has become unavoidable.

As Jeff Bezos put it, "AI is ... a horizontal enabling layer. It can be used to improve everything. It will be in everything."

(Medium, 'Jeff Bezos Nails the AI Story', Dec. 2024)

The Strategic Shift

But here is the critical point: **AI itself is not the strategy.** The real power lies in the data that fuels it. Without quality, connected, and well-governed data, AI becomes just another automation tool—fast, but shallow. Too many organizations still operate in silos, where information is fragmented, duplicated, and underutilized. Innovation stalls. Risks remain hidden. Processes slow down. The challenge is not adopting AI; it is building intelligence from data.

This shift is not about chasing technology for its own sake. It is about connecting the dots between people, processes, and information. Data is not just fuel for AI. It is intelligence, created, owned, and used by people. It gains value only when paired with human judgment, context, and action.

The Opportunity Beyond Efficiency

For leaders, investors, and decision-makers, this perspective unlocks a bigger opportunity. Companies that treat data as intelligence can do more than keep up with competitors. They can create ecosystems capable of solving pressing challenges—healthcare inequities, climate resilience, and financial inclusion—that no single organization can tackle alone.

As Satya Nadella has argued, "AI is going to be the key to understanding and solving many of the world's most complex problems."

(Time Magazine, '15 Quotes on the Future of AI, Apr. 2025)

WHY THIS PERSPECTIVE MATTERS

For more than two decades, I've worked at the intersection of business transformation, technology, and operations. My career has taken me across industries, from healthcare and medical devices to financial services to consumer products and enterprise technology. In every environment, the same pattern emerged: data was everywhere, but insight was rare.

I began with hard skills. Accounting and finance trained me to see where dollars moved, while Lean Six Sigma sharpened my eye for inefficiencies. Those tools helped me measure performance and design strategies that delivered results. Yet I quickly learned that transformation never succeeds on tools alone. Real change depends on people, how they interpret the data, how they collaborate, and how they make decisions together.

That truth became clear in high-stakes projects. On compliance initiatives, I saw how regulatory requirements weren't just checklists, but strategic levers that shaped entire portfolios. In digital transformation programs, I watched marketing, operations, and supply chain leaders finally connect their data and, in doing so, connect their teams. I learned that progress often hinged not on dashboards, but on dialogue.

One of my greatest lessons came from working across cultures and generations. The seasoned professional who understood a process inside and out. The new analyst willing to ask why things have always been done a certain way. The global colleague whose local context reframed a problem entirely. Data alone could not deliver those perspectives. It was the people who made the difference, and when they connected, the intelligence became powerful.

This is why I wrote this book. The conversation around artificial intelligence dominates headlines, but too little attention is given to the intelligence already inside organizations. It sits in the judgment of employees closest to the work, in the tacit knowledge that connects finance to operations, and in the lived experiences that give meaning to numbers. AI has a role to play, but it will fail without this foundation.

My aim is to equip leaders, investors, and future decision-makers with a new way to see data: not as raw inputs for machines, but as the connective tissue that aligns people, processes, and strategy. The lessons ahead are drawn not from theory, but from practice. From moments where silos created risk, and from the breakthroughs that happened when teams connected the dots.

The message is simple: transformation is not about chasing the latest platform. It is about harnessing the intelligence you already have—**your people, your data, your context**—and using it to shape what comes next.

BRIDGE TO PART 1 – FROM PERSPECTIVE TO PRACTICE

You now know where my perspective comes from: years of working across industries and solving problems that were as much about people as they were about processes or platforms. The most important lesson was always the same. Data only becomes powerful when it is connected, contextual, and shaped by human judgment.

But awareness alone doesn't change anything. If we want to build organizations that actually use intelligence well, we need to start with the foundation. That means understanding the current landscape: what kinds of data exist, what happens when they remain siloed, and why human context determines whether information becomes noise or insight.

That's where Part 1 begins.

PART 1

Understanding the Landscape

CHAPTER 1

BREAKING DOWN SILOS FOR GROWTH

Most organizations don't fail because of a lack of data. They fail because their data is trapped. Finance looks at costs, marketing looks at campaigns, HR looks at attrition, and each believes they see the truth. In reality, they're staring at fragments of a larger story. When information is isolated in silos, collaboration slows, blind spots expand, and opportunities for growth quietly slip away.

I learned this early in my career, when I was asked to review customer survey comments. At the time, our internal metric for success was "speed to answer," and the dashboard proudly displayed green. But when I compared it to customer feedback, the truth came out: customers didn't care how fast we said hello; they cared how long it took to solve their problem. Our cases averaged three days to close, and a quarter of them had to be reopened. The survey data was there all along, but because no one connected it to operational metrics, we were celebrating the wrong thing. That is what silos do. They make you optimize locally while missing what matters globally.

These silos show up everywhere. Marketing runs campaigns without knowing whether they improve long-term retention. Operations manages vendor scorecards, while finance only feels the pain when costs appear months later. HR monitors attrition but struggles to connect it to stalled innovation. Customer service collects feedback that never makes it to product design. Each team is doing its job, but without integration, the organization loses the ability to innovate or respond to change.

The consequences are real. I once worked on a compliance case where quality data lived in one system, regulatory updates in another, and financial impacts in a third. No one had a joined view. By the time leadership understood the full picture, remediation costs were piling up. The signals had been visible all along, but they were not visible in the same room at the same time.

And silos don't just create risk; they stall growth. At a financial services firm, the "head of household" was assumed to be the only investor worth tracking. That meant spouses, adult children, and parents—the very people influencing financial decisions—were invisible. Once data was connected across systems, whole new segments emerged. Growth opportunities didn't have to be invented; they were simply uncovered.

Why Breaking Silos Matters Now

Breaking down silos isn't just about saving time or eliminating duplication. It is about building something far greater. At its core, it is about creating insight, the ability to see beyond narrow departmental metrics and understand how the enterprise is performing as a whole. It is about enabling collaboration, giving teams the space and trust to share intelligence rather than guard it. And it is about resilience—the strength to respond to disruption with speed and clarity, because the full picture is finally visible.

In a world where every decision is shaped by data, the organizations that thrive will be those that stop treating data as isolated departmental assets and start seeing it as an enterprise-wide intelligence system.

For leaders, this raises some uncomfortable but necessary questions. Can your customer-facing teams see the same information that your finance and product teams are using? Are regulatory requirements visible across systems, or do they still depend on manual reconciliation? How many of today's decisions are made on incomplete or siloed information? And if a disruption hit tomorrow, how quickly could your organization respond if your teams were not all working from the same intelligence?

Breaking silos is not just about cleaning up processes or saving time. It is about insight: the ability to see the enterprise as a whole. It is about resilience: the ability to respond quickly because the full picture is visible. And it is about trust: delivering on promises to customers because the left hand finally knows what the right hand is doing.

The lesson is simple. Data only becomes intelligence when it is connected. A green metric in one silo can hide a red experience for the customer across the whole journey. Leaders who make these connections, who bring finance, operations, customer service, product, and compliance into the same conversation, gain more than efficiency. They gain the ability to see risks before they escalate, opportunities before they are obvious, and customers as they actually experience the organization.

So the question for leaders is this: Where in your organization are you still celebrating siloed green lights while missing the red flags across the entire journey?

CHAPTER 2

THE COST OF IGNORING DATA

The Data Dilemma: What's Really Holding Companies Back

AI is on everyone's lips today, but beneath the buzz lies a hard truth: no algorithm, no matter how advanced, can deliver value without the right data. And for most organizations, that remains the greatest obstacle.

Businesses run on a patchwork of systems. Customer Relationship Management (CRM) handles client interactions. Enterprise Resource Planning (ERP) covers financials. Product Lifecycle Management (PLM) drives design. Human Resource Information Systems (HRIS) track talent. In healthcare, it's Electronic Health Records (EHR). On top of all that, there are spreadsheets, third-party apps, and point solutions. Each of these systems works fine on its own, but together they form a disjointed puzzle.

The result is familiar. Teams make decisions with partial information. Finance pulls quarterly numbers that lag behind reality. Operations watches shipments but doesn't connect them to revenue impact until it's too late. Marketing measures campaigns but can't see if they drive loyalty. HR tracks attrition without connecting it to delivery delays or innovation slowdowns. Everyone has a piece, but no one sees the whole picture.

This fragmentation is more than frustrating. It's expensive. It slows decisions, hides risks, and makes organizations reactive instead of proactive. I've watched leaders explain profitability on investor calls as though it were solely tied to global forces, such as optimism, inflation, or regulatory pressure. But inside the company, the real story was often smaller and more specific: products that weren't pulling their weight, customers quietly churning, or costs compounding because nobody had connected the dots across functions.

Product portfolios are a perfect example. A low-revenue product might look like a distraction, but it could also represent a valuable niche that deserves investment. Without connecting finance, sales, and operations data, companies can't answer basic questions: Is the cost worth it? Is there a better substitute? Or should we reallocate resources? Too often, these conversations never happen because the data that would fuel them lives in different silos.

Customer support tells the same story. Organizations handle the same complaints over and over. Buried in those tickets are patterns that reveal design flaws or process gaps. But unless those insights are shared beyond the support team, they are wasted. The price shows up in longer calls, frustrated customers, and lost trust.

This is where the temptation to leap into AI pilots becomes dangerous. Chatbots, copilots, predictive engines—all of it sounds exciting. But when these tools lack access to clean, connected data, they collapse into little more than automation. They answer without insight. They react without learning. They deliver speed without direction.

Brian Marshall of Citi put it bluntly: "AI without data is like life without oxygen." And Florian Douetteau, CEO of Dataiku, went further: "Messy, siloed data—now, with the urgency to deploy effective AI, fixing it isn't just essential, it's existential."

(Reuters, 'Unglamourous world of 'data infrastructure' driving hot tech M & A market in AI race, Jul. 2025)

The numbers bear this out. A Reltio survey found that more than ninety percent of organizations believe breaking silos would improve AI performance, but only twenty-one percent say their initiatives are delivering results. *(Reltio, 'Enterprise data leaders our AI ambitions are stalling out on silos', Dec. 2024)*

McKinsey estimates the annual cost of siloed data at over three trillion dollars worldwide in lost productivity and missed opportunity. *(Forbes, "Why removing data silos is key to unlocking AI value", Feb. 2025)* That number is staggering, but most people don't need a global statistic to understand the impact. They live it every day in the rework, reconciliation, and second-guessing that comes with incomplete information.

The real irony is that while companies rush to buy AI solutions, many can't answer basic operational questions with confidence. Which products drive satisfaction and which cause churn? Where exactly do costs spiral? How long does it truly take to resolve a customer issue, from the first call to final fix? These are not AI questions. They are business questions. And without integrated, reliable data, no tool, no matter how advanced, can answer them well.

I once joined a project where leaders were eager to test predictive models, but when we asked for historical data to train them, we discovered that definitions didn't match across systems. "Active customer" meant one thing to finance, another to marketing, and something entirely different to service. The models produced elegant dashboards, but they weren't aligned to reality. The problem wasn't the algorithm. It was the lack of shared understanding of the data itself.

Data is not just a technical detail in the back office. It is either a strategic asset or a liability. When it is ignored, organizations pay twice: once in direct inefficiency and again in missed opportunity. AI makes the stakes higher because it amplifies whatever you give it. Feed it clean, connected data with context, and it can transform your business. Feed it siloed, messy data, and it will scale confusion at breathtaking speed.

The lesson is clear. Ignoring data is not just a technical oversight; it is a strategic risk. Leaders who fail to recognize this will keep running faster on the wrong track, while those who invest in connecting data will find themselves not just keeping up, but moving ahead.

CHAPTER 3

DATA IS HUMAN-CENTRIC

Reframing the Textbook View

At its core, data is not an abstract asset; it is a tangible resource. It is generated by people, curated by people, and interpreted by people. Every transaction, survey response, or system entry represents a human decision or action. What transforms those raw numbers into intelligence isn't the system that stores them, but the context and judgment applied by the people closest to the work.

Yet in many organizations, this truth gets lost. Leaders talk about "big data" or "AI" as though intelligence emerges automatically from volume or processing power. In reality, intelligence is created at the intersection of human expertise and data context. Strip away the human element, and data is little more than a box of puzzle pieces without a picture on the cover. It's technically complete, but impossible to assemble into anything meaningful.

Who Creates and Curates Data?

The people who create and curate data span every level of the organization. Frontline employees log customer tickets, sales reps enter deal details, and clinicians document patient outcomes. Subject matter experts add interpretation, supply chain managers spot disruption signals, compliance officers track regulatory requirements, and engineers convert test results into design improvements. Leaders then connect the dots across functions, seeing how workforce patterns affect innovation, or how customer feedback influences financial performance. Each layer adds meaning. Without it, data is just noise.

I saw this in a program involving networked devices. Support teams were mostly reactive, responding after outages had already frustrated customers. But a few field technicians noticed something subtle: minor error codes often appeared days before a major failure. By connecting these dots—logs, install environments, and ticket history—they showed that data could be used predictively, not just reactively. It wasn't the system that caught this pattern; it was human expertise applied to data in context.

Why Context Matters

The same data point can mean very different things depending on who is looking at it. A dip in customer usage might suggest dissatisfaction to marketing, but operations might see it as a looming capacity issue. A series of late shipments could look like a supplier reliability problem to procurement, but finance may see it as a cash-flow issue. Even employee attrition looks different depending on where you sit: HR may view it as a retention challenge, while R&D sees it as a hit to innovation capacity. Context is what turns a number into a decision.

Sometimes, the problem is the assumption built into the system itself. I worked with a financial services firm that designed its customer journeys around the "head of household," assuming that one person was the primary investor. In practice, spouses, adult children, and even parents all played active roles in decision-making. By focusing on a single role, the company ignored entire segments of influence. Once we broadened the journey to reflect everyone at the table, opportunities that had been invisible suddenly appeared.

The lesson here is that context changes everything. Without it, organizations risk acting on narrow or misleading interpretations of the data. I saw this again in a compliance initiative. Regulatory updates required more frequent patient safety disclosures. Compliance teams viewed the change as non-negotiable. Finance saw only the rising costs and questioned whether the investment was justified. It wasn't until compliance leaders explained the regulatory stakes in full that finance recalibrated. What initially looked like a discretionary line item became a strategic requirement once context was shared.

Human Judgment as the Differentiator

This is why human judgment remains the differentiator. Machines can surface patterns at speed and scale, but they cannot weigh cultural nuance in a workforce trend, interpret emotion in a customer's voice, or anticipate how regulators might respond to an evolving gray area. AI can tell you that customer sentiment is dropping, but only a person can determine whether that drop signals frustration, confusion, or simply seasonal behavior.

I once watched a product team celebrate what looked like a success: the dashboard was green, the launch was on time, on budget, and all planned features were delivered. But adoption lagged, and customer satisfaction plummeted. Support calls spiked. What the data showed was execution. What it didn't show was relevance. Customers no longer needed the features that were built. What looked like a win on paper was actually a miss in practice. The numbers alone didn't tell the story.

And sometimes the story is painfully human. Imagine an elderly customer who has just lost their spouse. They call a financial institution for help accessing benefits. The system is designed for efficiency: documents are listed, online portals are available 24/7, and the call center script is optimized. On paper, everything works. But to the customer, the process feels overwhelming. The forms are confusing, the automated menu doesn't understand their accent, and every interaction adds frustration at a time of grief. The system may record "case resolved." What it misses is the distress the person experienced along the way.

These gaps appear in every industry. Healthcare data may show a lab value within range, but only a clinician knows that, in combination with a patient's history, it signals something urgent. Financial algorithms may flag an anomaly, but it takes a risk manager to know whether it is fraud or simply an unusual but legitimate purchase. Manufacturing sensors may detect a variation, but only an experienced quality engineer can decide if it is within tolerance or cause for concern.

Across projects I've led, the turning point is rarely the dashboard itself. It is when we bring the right people together to ask, "What does this mean?" Aligning perspectives often exposes assumptions that no single function would have caught alone. Data doesn't change, but the understanding of it does.

Ultimately, data is not about numbers alone. It is about the people who create it, the context in which it exists, and the decisions it informs. Too often, employees only see the metrics assigned to their own function, without understanding how those numbers connect to enterprise goals, such as customer retention, innovation capacity, or compliance integrity. That isn't ignorance; it is a design flaw.

What would change if everyone understood not only their own data, but how it fit into the larger story? In the intelligence era, organizations that keep this truth at the center—data as human, contextual, and purposeful—will be the ones best positioned to thrive. Machines can scale patterns, but only people can decide what those patterns mean.

As I look back on the projects where data became more than numbers, the common thread was always people. The analysts, frontline teams, and specialists closest to the signals had the clearest view of what mattered. The real challenge for leaders is to make sure those voices are not only heard but amplified. It means asking yourself hard questions: Who in your organization is closest to the data, and how often are they invited into decision-making? Where are assumptions being made without human review? What insights are lost when teams work in isolation? And most importantly, how do you design AI tools not to replace human judgment, but to elevate it?

BRIDGE FROM PART 1 TO PART 2 – TURNING INSIGHT INTO ACTION

We've mapped the environment. We've seen the many faces of data, the costs of ignoring it, and the truth that intelligence is always human-centric. But knowing the problem is only half the battle.

Progress requires that teams and processes be designed for change. It means moving beyond dashboards into the messiness of cross-functional work. It means having executives aligned on outcomes, employees empowered to ask questions, and data turned into a shared language across the organization.

Part 2 is about building that machinery.

PART 2

Building Teams and Processes for Intelligence

CHAPTER 4

ASSEMBLING TEAMS FOR TRANSFORMATION

Transformation often begins with a deceptively simple question: Is there a better way? A better way to design a product, to organize teams, to measure outcomes. It rarely starts with technology. It begins with curiosity.

Seeing the Whole Picture

Most companies have familiar scorecards: financial performance, compliance, customer experience metrics like Net Promoter Score. Leaders track these measures quarter after quarter; exceptions get flagged, trends get discussed, and reports are shared. But in my experience, transformation doesn't start in the boardroom review. It starts when someone notices something doesn't add up and decides to dig deeper.

I remember one morning when the operations dashboard looked calm. At 9:05, everything appeared green. At 9:07, a manager spotted a "one-time charge" that had actually shown up six times.

At 9:10, someone asked, "Can we get finance, service, and product in the same room today?" That's how transformation really starts. Not with a glossy presentation, but with a group of people realizing that what one function calls an exception is actually a recurring pattern with broad impact.

In this case, the "one-time charges" turned out to be expedited shipments of replacement parts. Operations traced them to a faulty component. Supplier Quality launched a root-cause investigation. Finance measured the cost impact. Sales prepared proactive outreach to customers to protect trust. It became clear that no single team could resolve the issue in isolation. The solution required perspectives from across the company. And once the pattern was visible, leaders expanded the scorecard to track supplier performance and introduced multi-sourcing for critical parts.

That experience taught me that data becomes intelligence when it is examined by people who see the world from different perspectives. What finance considers an expense, operations might recognize as a signal. What customer service calls a complaint, product design may view as an insight. Sometimes the most powerful thing you can do is simply gather a cross-functional team and have them look at the same data together.

Balancing Today and Tomorrow

In nearly every transformation I've led, the work began with two essential lenses in the room: those who deeply understood how the process worked today, and those who could imagine how it should work tomorrow. The tension between these groups is what creates momentum. One side grounds ideas in practical realities, the other pushes for possibilities beyond the current limits. Neither perspective is enough on its own.

But building these teams is not easy. People worry. Will this mean more work? Will my job disappear? Will we just create new problems downstream? Anxiety is natural, and if it isn't addressed, it becomes resistance. That is why mapping upstream and downstream impacts is so important. Fixing one part of a process can create ripple effects elsewhere, and the team has to be honest about those trade-offs.

I've often been asked to lead programs with nothing more than a goal and a budget. There was no detailed script, no roadmap neatly prepared in advance. It felt like writing the menu while the dinner rush had already started. When vision ran ahead of execution, we wasted time on rework. When execution sprinted without vision, we hit milestones that didn't matter. The real work was balancing both: thinkers who challenged assumptions, and doers who tested reality early.

The strongest teams are built around journeys, not org charts. If the journey touches the customer, then service must be in the room. If the journey involves product features, engineering needs a voice. If the journey has cost implications, finance must weigh in. Legal defines boundaries, IT ensures integration, and data teams link signals across systems. Not everyone has equal weight in every decision, but leaving out a key perspective almost guarantees costly surprises later.

Shared outcomes are what align these teams. When each function measures only its own KPIs, behaviors remain siloed. When the whole group rallies around outcomes like time to value, customer effort, or unit economics, trade-offs become transparent. Suddenly, a decision is no longer about one department winning; it is about the enterprise moving forward.

Outcomes Leaders as Orchestrators

Orchestration is the other key. Even the best cross-functional teams need someone to connect the dots and guide decision-making. In my experience, this role is less about hierarchy and more about translation. I call it the Outcomes Leader. This person makes decision rights explicit, surfaces trade-offs, and keeps the focus on what matters most: the customer and the business. They don't just facilitate. They take responsibility for how decisions get made.

I once watched an Outcomes Leader save a launch meeting from spiraling into conflict. Operations wanted more checkpoints, Marketing wanted to go live immediately, and Legal flagged compliance concerns. Rather than force a consensus, the Outcomes Leader reframed the debate: which changes were reversible this week, and which were irreversible later? The team shipped a reversible update immediately, queued the irreversible items for legal review, and documented who owned what. Nobody got everything they wanted, but the customer got a better experience, and momentum wasn't lost.

Strong Outcomes Leaders don't need rare credentials. They often emerge from product managers who ship across functions, operations leaders who manage value streams, finance professionals who think in unit economics, or program leaders who deliver real change rather than polished slides. They also carry a future lens, mapping what skills will be needed, what guardrails make AI safe, and how incentives must evolve to reward outcomes instead of throughput.

Evolving Program Management

This kind of orchestration points to a larger shift organizations must make. Traditional Program Management Offices often sit inside one silo, answering to the budget that funds them. As a result, priorities are filtered through local incentives. To lead true transformation, the PMO itself must evolve into a transformation office. It must be neutral, cross-functional, and anchored to outcomes that serve the entire enterprise. Only then can dashboards become more than a set of numbers. They become living tools in the hands of teams who know how to act on them.

That is the real truth of transformation: dashboards don't change companies. Teams do. And the best teams are assembled not around structures, but around journeys, outcomes, and leaders who know how to turn intent into impact.

CHAPTER 5

DATA ANALYSIS FOR INSIGHTFUL DECISIONS

Every organization has its rhythms. Quarterly business reviews, financial scorecards, operational dashboards. Sales gains and losses are reported by product or region. Profitability is summarized as the cost of sales. Customer satisfaction is boiled down to an index score. These measures have their place. They provide accountability and history, a way to track whether the business is broadly on course.

But those measures are rearview mirrors. They tell you what has happened, not why it happened or what is likely to come next. In the age of AI, descriptive metrics are table stakes. What propels organizations forward is analysis that digs deeper, challenges assumptions, and uncovers signals others have overlooked.

I once worked with a company that rolled out new digital tools so customers could place orders online or find answers faster. Leadership celebrated the launch, but questions soon followed. Were customers actually using the tools? Did they like the experience? Were problems being solved, or simply being shifted into different queues? Traditional reporting gave little clarity. Only when we began analyzing usage data, feedback, and service outcomes together did the real picture emerge: the tools were technically sound, but the onboarding process confused customers, creating new frustrations that offset the intended gains.

The same story plays out internally. Companies invest in training programs, measure completion rates, and declare success. Yet the question is not how many people finished the training, but whether it closed knowledge gaps, sped up delivery, or improved customer outcomes. Without deeper analysis, activity masquerades as progress.

The first step in moving beyond surface metrics is to recognize the three kinds of data that matter most. Financial data shows the impact on the bottom line: revenue, cost of sales, and profitability by product or market. Operational data shows how efficiently the organization is executing: supply chain performance, production throughput, fulfillment speed, and service resolution. Customer data shows who is being served and what they need: attributes, purchase history, digital engagement, feedback, and relationships.

Each of these views is valuable on its own. But intelligence lives at the intersection. When they remain siloed, decisions are made in narrow channels. Finance pushes margin improvement without visibility into customer sentiment. Operations streamlines processes that customers may not even value. Marketing personalizes campaigns but promises what supply chains cannot deliver profitably.

I saw this dynamic in something as ordinary as the cereal aisle. Customers enjoyed dozens of choices, each variation a symbol of abundance. From a marketing perspective, variety seemed like loyalty. From operations, it was complexity: more stock-keeping units, more sourcing, more packaging. From finance, many of those boxes barely broke even. Without connecting customer demand, operational feasibility, and financial contribution, the company couldn't tell whether variety was serving loyalty or simply creating waste.

Clarity also depends on how attributes are defined. "Active customer" might mean anyone with a balance to finance, but to marketing, it might mean someone who opened an email in the last ninety days. Both are technically correct, but unless they are aligned, the organization ends up building strategies on mismatched truths. AI models will happily scale those definitions, but if the foundations are inconsistent, the insights will be misleading.

The challenge is not unique to consumer goods. In healthcare, I worked on a platform that aimed to personalize benefits offerings. The idea was simple: deliver the right package at the right moment. In practice, finance struggled to model the risk, operations couldn't deliver onboarding quickly enough, and customer service spent its days apologizing. Only when financial, operational, and customer data were joined together did the personalization actually work. The results were dramatic: onboarding times improved, and new client acquisition rose by 25 percent. The data was always there, but until it was connected, it wasn't intelligence.

This is what distinguishes old-school reporting from intelligence in the AI era. Traditional metrics describe the past. Predictive and adaptive analysis shows what is likely to happen next and why. Instead of waiting for customer churn to appear in quarterly numbers, predictive models flag which customers are at risk, allowing leaders to act before it's too late. Instead of measuring training hours, analysis shows whether skills are actually being applied, and where coaching is needed. Instead of waiting for supplier delays to show up in cost overruns, data signals disruptions in advance, giving companies time to adapt.

From Rearview to Radar: How Metrics Evolve

Traditional reporting is like the rearview mirror. It tells you where you've been. AI-era insights act more like radar, showing what's ahead and flagging risks before they collide with the business.

Traditional Metrics	AI-Era Insights
Sales growth by product/region (quarterly)	Predictive customer lifetime value (CLV), churn probability
Net Promoter Score (survey-based)	Real-time sentiment analysis across digital channels
Cost of sales (summarized)	Unit economics, margin contribution by micro-segment
Training completion rates	Skill adoption curves, time-to-proficiency, knowledge gap closure
Supplier cost tracking	Supplier reliability scoring, predictive disruption alerts
Quarterly dashboards & exception reporting	Continuous monitoring, AI-driven alerts, agentic AI workflows

These comparisons highlight the difference between describing the past and anticipating the future. Companies that embrace AI-era analysis don't discard traditional measures; they expand them, using deeper insights to validate assumptions, surface risks earlier, and uncover opportunities that dashboards alone can't reveal.

The real shift happens when leaders stop treating metrics as a compliance exercise and start treating them as a decision-making compass. That requires different kinds of questions. Leaders should ask themselves whether financial, operational, and customer systems truly talk to each other or still report separately. They should ask whether personalization efforts are tied to what can be delivered profitably, or whether promises are being made that the organization cannot keep. They should examine how quickly shifting customer needs are reflected in financial forecasts and operational plans. They should consider whether they are measuring skill adoption, rather than just training completions. And they should interrogate recurring issues in exception reports, asking whether these are surface-level anomalies or signals of deeper truths that have yet to be addressed.

But technology alone doesn't drive this shift. It takes leadership. In one initiative, we instituted a weekly "analysis session." It wasn't another dashboard review. We brought finance, operations, product, and customer experience leaders into the same room with a one-page joined view. We asked one question: if our fix is real, what should move first? That became the signal to watch. Each week, the team traced one handoff in detail, made a decision, and assigned ownership to it. Every two weeks, they demonstrated a real before-and-after. The process was simple, visible, and repeatable, but the impact was profound.

Leadership in this age means more than reading charts. It means interpreting them, connecting them, and challenging them. It means asking where the company is paying twice, where "one-time" charges keep repeating, and where survey themes point to root causes. It means knowing when AI is surfacing patterns and when humans must bring context. It means reducing noise, clarifying definitions, and focusing on the signals that truly matter.

I've learned that when cross-functional teams share a single joined view, the debates shift. Slide decks give way to real outcomes. Competing truths are replaced with shared facts. Surprises diminish because risk and compliance have been at the table from the start. Overloaded scorecards are replaced with a few leading and lagging signals that guide decisions.

Dashboards describe. Analysis explains. Intelligence predicts. The organizations that thrive will be those that connect financial, operational, and customer data into one shared intelligence system. Not to measure activity, but to anticipate risk, personalize experiences, and uncover opportunities others miss.

CHAPTER 6

MAPPING CUSTOMER EXPERIENCE

In Chapter 5, we explored how connecting financial, operational, and customer data creates intelligence. But spreadsheets and dashboards only tell part of the story. To truly understand where breakdowns occur, leaders need to walk in the shoes of their customers, employees, and partners. That is where journey mapping comes in.

Turning Journeys Into Stories

A journey map turns data into a story. It traces how people move through interactions, where handoffs succeed or fail, and where promises are kept or broken. It is one thing to know that abandonment rates are high. It is another to see the moment at 9:15 a.m. when a customer uploads the same document for the third time, at 9:17 when the support queue groans, and at 9:20 when intake sends them back to step one. A journey map makes that loop visible, and with one small change in the process, the "frequent flyer" complaint disappears.

Why Connection, Not Features, Drives Experience

Organizations often assume that improving experience means adding features or channels. But most friction is not about more; it is about connection. A customer may click through beautifully designed marketing content, yet struggle to complete an order online. An employee may finish required training, yet lack the tools to apply what they learned. A supplier may deliver on time, yet because performance data never reaches finance, hidden costs accumulate. The map exposes these disconnects. It forces leaders to see not only what their departments report, but what the end-to-end experience feels like to the person living it.

When data is layered onto journeys, the connections become even clearer. Financial data shows whether behaviors strengthen or erode profitability. Operational data highlights bottlenecks that stall progress. Customer data reveals whether experiences feel personal or generic. Together, the three views transform a flowchart into intelligence.

I once worked on a healthcare initiative that looked straightforward: symptoms, visit, scheduling, surgery, and follow-up. But the real insight came when we overlaid the three data types. On the customer side, we captured expectations and emotions, including anxiety over symptoms, reassurance after the visit, and clarity at follow-up. On the operational side, we tracked cycle times, pre-authorization delays, and care-team handoffs. On the financial side, we saw denial rates, expedite costs, and readmission penalties. With all three together, trade-offs became visible. Cutting days off the pre-authorization step added cost to processing, but it reduced cancellations, which were far more expensive and damaging to trust.

Patterns like this emerge across industries. Onboarding promises speed, but silos create delays. Service teams capture valuable feedback, but product teams rarely see it in real-time. Supply chains signal disruptions, but finance recognizes the costs only after the fact. Marketing personalizes campaigns, but fulfillment cannot deliver on the promises. Each breakdown is more than inefficiency—it is a moment where trust erodes, cost rises, and opportunity is lost.

And journeys are not limited to customers. Suppliers, distributors, and partners also experience the organization. A supplier may deliver on time, yet mismatched invoicing creates costly reconciliation. A distributor without inventory visibility misses commitments. A regulator demands reports, yet inconsistent data collection creates compliance risks. These journeys ripple back into customer satisfaction, financial outcomes, and brand trust.

What excites me most is the potential of ecosystem journeys. Inside a single company, journey maps reveal connections. But imagine what happens when industries map journeys together. Healthcare providers, insurers, regulators, and manufacturers could share views of the patient journey, identifying inefficiencies that no single player could see alone. Retailers, logistics providers, and producers could build a real-time view of supply chains. The barriers—privacy, competition, regulation—are real. But so is the potential for better outcomes if journeys extend beyond organizational walls.

From Description to Orchestration

Journey mapping is not about drawing pretty diagrams. It is about orchestration. When linked to live data, a journey map becomes predictive, not just descriptive. Friction can be detected in real-time, personalization can be adjusted dynamically, and employees and partners can see how their piece contributes to the whole.

The lesson is clear: dashboards describe, but journeys reveal. They show the truth of how people actually experience the organization, not just how leaders hope they do. And when combined with data across financial, operational, and customer dimensions, they become a powerful tool for redesigning processes, rebuilding trust, and delivering on the promise of intelligence.

BRIDGE FROM PART 2 TO PART 3 – FROM FOUNDATION TO STRATEGY

With the right teams in place and processes designed for intelligence, the question shifts: how do we actually apply all of this?

This is where strategy comes in. Breakdowns aren't just problems to fix. They're signals of opportunity. AI isn't just another tool. It's a collaborator. And platforms? They only work if process and context come first.

Part 3 explores what it means to apply intelligence strategically, to avoid the common traps, and to put humans and machines to work together in ways that truly transform.

PART 3

Applying Intelligence Strategically

CHAPTER 7

EVALUATING BREAKDOWNS AND OPPORTUNITIES

In Chapter 6, we saw how journey mapping reveals the places where promises fall apart, handoffs fail, and trust erodes. Those breakdowns can feel discouraging at first—like evidence that the system is broken. But I have learned, time and again, that breakdowns are not just failures. They are signals. They point directly to the opportunities that matter most.

When I was working on a product-to-service transformation, the breakdowns came fast and often. A system designed for shipping physical goods struggled when service offerings were added. Support teams found themselves chasing tickets through disconnected tools. Sales teams promised outcomes that the back office wasn't ready to deliver. At first, it felt like chaos. But as we examined each breakdown, patterns emerged. They showed us exactly where the processes needed to evolve, which systems required integration, and where employee training had to shift. What looked like failure was actually the roadmap for change.

This is true across industries. A delayed handoff in a hospital is not only a patient risk; it is a signal that communication between departments needs repair. A spike in customer complaints about onboarding is not just noise; it is a signal that expectations and processes are misaligned. A compliance failure is not only a legal problem; it is a signal that upstream data collection is incomplete or inconsistent.

The hardest part for leaders is resisting the temptation to treat breakdowns as isolated events to patch and move on. A missed shipment here, a lost ticket there, a frustrated employee who leaves—it is tempting to fix the symptom and declare success. But if the same types of issues keep appearing, they are telling you something deeper. They reveal where silos hold too much power, where processes are brittle, and where people lack the support to succeed.

Transformations are hard because breakdowns are inevitable. They surface the tension between the old way of working and the new way that is being built. They demand patience, persistence, and resilience. I remember being in rooms where every participant was frustrated, defensive, or exhausted by the effort. Yet those moments, uncomfortable as they were, gave us the richest insights. They forced us to ask: What is this breakdown really showing us? What truth about our systems, our culture, or our customer commitments is coming to the surface?

When breakdowns are reframed as signals, organizations begin to see them differently. They become less about blame and more about discovery. Less about short-term fixes and more about long-term opportunity. They mark the places where leaders must lean in, not only to solve the problem but to strengthen the system around it.

Breakdowns are not the enemy of transformation. They are the teachers. They show us where resilience must be built, where trust must be repaired, and where the next breakthrough is waiting.

Prioritizing Breakdowns for Action

A simple matrix can help leaders move from "everything is a problem" to "here is what matters most."

Type of Breakdown	Cost of Inaction	Opportunity Potential	AI Enablement Potential
Customer Experience	High (trust erosion)	High (loyalty, upsell)	Strong (sentiment analysis, personalization)
Operational Efficiency	Medium (resource drain)	High (automation, scale)	Strong (Robotic Process Automation/RPA, predictive ops)
Compliance/ Regulation	High (fines, market risk)	Medium (risk reduction)	Strong (monitoring, traceability)
Partner/ Supplier	Medium (delays, cost)	High (resilience, agility)	Medium (risk scoring, forecasting)

By evaluating breakdowns against cost, opportunity, and AI potential, leaders can prioritize where to act, where to experiment, and where to pause.

The real work for leaders is not simply fixing breakdowns as they appear, but asking the deeper questions they expose. Which recurring issues reveal truths we have avoided? Are we solving surface problems quickly or addressing root causes with discipline? Do our silos still create friction that no amount of automation can erase? Are we learning from breakdowns, or hiding them out of fear? And most importantly, what criteria guide us in deciding which problems matter most for the future of our business?

These questions turn breakdowns into a strategic compass. They shift the mindset from firefighting to foresight, from patching cracks to reinforcing the foundation. The leaders who treat breakdowns as teachers will uncover resilience where others see fragility, opportunity where others see obstacles, and intelligence where others see only noise.

CHAPTER 8

HUMAN + MACHINE COLLABORATION

In Chapter 7, we reframed breakdowns as signals: not just problems to solve, but opportunities that point the way forward. The question then becomes, how do organizations respond? More and more, the answer lies in how humans and machines learn to work together.

Artificial intelligence brings extraordinary strengths. It can scan vast amounts of data in seconds, spot patterns invisible to human eyes, and run twenty-four hours a day without pause. But intelligence is more than pattern recognition. It is context. It is meaning. It is judgment. These are distinctly human strengths, and they cannot be programmed into an algorithm. The organizations that thrive are those that see AI not as a substitute for people, but as an amplifier of their capability.

I saw this firsthand while working with a financial services team that was drowning in exception reports. AI models could flag anomalies instantly, transactions that seemed out of place, and sudden changes in customer behavior. But those alerts were only useful when analysts stepped in to interpret them. Was the anomaly a case of fraud, or a loyal customer making a large purchase? The AI could raise the question, but only people with experience, intuition, and accountability could provide the answer. Together, they achieved a level of efficiency and accuracy that neither side could have reached alone.

The same lesson appears in healthcare. Diagnostic models can highlight irregularities on a scan faster than any radiologist. Yet, a machine cannot sit with a patient, explain the findings, and weigh treatment options in the context of family history or lifestyle. AI may point to possibilities, but only human clinicians can make decisions grounded in empathy and ethics. It is not man versus machine; it is man with machine, each playing to their strengths.

When this collaboration is well-designed, operational excellence follows. Demand forecasting becomes sharper when algorithms project future needs and humans apply market context. Supply chains become more resilient when AI identifies disruption risks and leaders decide how to rebalance sourcing. Employee development accelerates when AI tracks learning curves and managers step in to mentor and coach. Again and again, the pattern repeats: AI extends capacity, but humans extend context.

This balance also matters beyond the enterprise. Climate scientists use AI to model environmental change at an unprecedented scale; however, it is policymakers and communities who decide how to act. Global supply chains rely on predictive models to forecast delays, but resilience only comes when governments, companies, and Non-Governmental Organizations (NGO) collaborate on solutions. The most pressing problems of our time—disease, inequality, and sustainability—will not be solved by machines alone. They demand human wisdom, amplified by machine insight.

I have learned that collaboration between humans and AI also reshapes the role of expertise. It is not enough to be an expert within your silo. A compliance officer must understand how customer data flows across departments. A product manager must grasp the implications of supplier disruptions. A marketer must know how influencer-driven content shapes demand signals. AI thrives on connected data, and so must the people who work with it. Subject matter expertise has to stretch across boundaries, linking functions that once operated in isolation.

Even as machines become more capable, there remain areas where human oversight is non-negotiable. Ethical decisions, accountability, and the interpretation of nuance cannot be delegated to code. A grieving customer cannot be reduced to a dataset. A sudden geopolitical shift cannot be explained by historical averages. Responsibility always rests with people, no matter how advanced the system.

AI Extends Reach, Humans Provide Purpose

Human and machine collaboration is not about handing over the wheel. It is about building workflows where each plays to its strength, creating intelligence that is both faster and wiser. Done well, this collaboration transforms breakdowns into breakthroughs. It strengthens not only companies but industries, and it equips leaders to address challenges far beyond the balance sheet.

The lesson is clear: AI extends reach, but people provide purpose. Together, they create a kind of collaborative intelligence that is greater than either one alone. The organizations that master this balance will not only move faster, they will move wiser. In doing so, they will lead the way into a future where intelligence is measured not just by machines, but by the human judgment that guides them.

CHAPTER 9

AVOIDING THE AI TRAP

In Chapter 8, we saw how humans and machines can complement each other: AI extends capacity while humans extend context. But what happens when that balance tips too far? What happens when organizations lean too heavily on technology, assuming algorithms alone can carry the weight of intelligence? That is where they stumble into the AI Trap.

The AI Trap is seductive. It promises speed, scale, and automation. Leaders hear about breakthroughs and rush to deploy them, convinced that simply having AI in place signals innovation. But the trap comes when AI is treated as a decision-maker rather than a decision-support tool. Without human oversight, bias creeps in unnoticed, compliance gaps widen, and strategies drift away from the reality of customer needs.

I recall working with a team that had just rolled out a new automation tool. The system was designed to accelerate customer approvals, and on paper, it looked like a success. But weeks later, complaints began to rise. The model was optimized for speed, not fairness, and it had quietly deprioritized entire segments of customers. What looked like progress was actually erosion of trust. The team had fallen into the trap of assuming the algorithm knew best.

The recent wave of large language models has only heightened this risk. These models are remarkable in their fluency. They can generate content that sounds authoritative, relevant, and human-like. But fluency is not accuracy. At their core, these models are statistical prediction engines. They predict the most likely sequence of words given a prompt. They are not databases of fact, reasoning systems, or sources of truth. They remix patterns drawn from the data they have been trained on. Without experts to frame the right questions, validate the results, and apply meaning, they can produce answers that sound right but are dangerously wrong.

This is why human expertise remains indispensable. Subject matter knowledge cannot be confined to a single silo. In the AI era, the marketing team needs to understand how influencer content shapes demand signals. Compliance teams need to know how data definitions ripple through customer experiences. Finance leaders must see not only numbers, but the attributes feeding those numbers. If a term like "customer value" or "head of household" is defined loosely, the model will reflect that looseness. The safeguard isn't fear; it is governance: clear definitions, fresh data, and alignment across functions so that when AI scales, it scales the right insights.

The AI Trap also shows up in more subtle ways. Sometimes it is chasing hype, deploying AI because competitors are doing it, without tying it to business outcomes. Sometimes it is overgeneralization, expecting AI to solve ill-defined problems, leaving technical teams scrambling to meet unclear requirements. And sometimes it is neglecting human context altogether, overlooking the insights of employees who are closest to the customer and the work itself. In each case, the risk is the same: decisions that look fast but prove shallow, efficient in the moment but costly in the long run.

I consider influencer-driven marketing to be one of the newest and most complex examples. Social media platforms generate torrents of data that feed into AI-driven recommendation systems. But what happens if organizations treat that data as a perfect signal of customer demand, without asking who is being influenced, by what, and to what end? The risk is building a strategy on noise, mistaking clicks for loyalty, and engagement for trust. Here again, human judgment matters. Someone has to connect the dots between what the algorithm highlights and what the customer actually values.

For executives and boards, the AI Trap is not a technical issue, but a leadership one. The responsibility is to frame problems clearly, to measure outcomes that matter, and to keep accountability where it belongs: with people, not machines. Vendors may provide powerful tools, but no vendor carries the responsibility for how those tools are used. That responsibility never leaves the boardroom.

Wisdom Can't Be Automated

The truth is that avoiding the AI Trap is not about rejecting AI, but about using it wisely. Large language models, predictive systems, and agentic AI can all be copilots, but they are not pilots. They can accelerate discovery, automate routine tasks, and surface patterns worth exploring. But only humans can provide the judgment, creativity, and accountability that turn those patterns into meaningful progress.

The greatest risk with AI is not what it cannot do; rather, the greatest risk is what people believe it can do. When leaders mistake fluency for truth, or speed for strategy, they surrender the very judgment that makes them valuable. The organizations that will thrive in the intelligence era are those that resist the trap, embrace human expertise, and use AI as an amplifier of intelligence rather than a replacement for it.

That balance—machine for scale; human for wisdom—is what ensures progress remains both fast and right.

CHAPTER 10

PROCESS BEFORE PLATFORM

When organizations begin exploring AI, the instinct is often to start with the technology. A new platform appears on the market, a vendor promises transformative results, and leaders feel the urgency to "bring it in" quickly. But technology alone does not transform. Platforms only create value when they are aligned to clearly defined problems, measurable requirements, and a process that people can follow.

Define Before You Deploy

I have seen what happens when this order is reversed. One financial services team I worked with faced long loan application times. Customers were frustrated, abandonment rates were climbing, and leadership was under pressure to fix it. The reflex could have been to buy the latest AI-driven workflow platform, but instead, the CIO made a different choice. He convened a cross-functional discovery team of loan officers, compliance managers, IT staff, and customer service reps, and asked them to map the process step by step. What emerged was eye-opening. Redundant document requests and manual compliance checks were slowing everything down. The people living the process every day already knew where the friction was. Once those requirements were clarified, vendors were brought in. This time, their solutions were pointed at the real problem, not at a vague hope of efficiency.

I've witnessed similar dynamics in healthcare. A technology company was eager to deploy AI chatbots to improve patient support, but the first step wasn't to buy the platform. It was to define the real problem. Patients weren't frustrated by the lack of features; they were frustrated by long wait times and inconsistent answers. The business requirement became clear: reduce response time, ensure accuracy of benefits information, and maintain compliance with HIPAA. Helpful. Correct. Compliant. Once that framing was in place, AI became part of the solution rather than the shiny distraction.

Manufacturing offers another lesson. A global company rushed into predictive maintenance because the CEO heard about it at a conference. Within months, money was pouring into a fast-tracked RFP. But implementation dragged. Why? Because no one had asked the right questions first. What mattered most: reduced outages, worker safety, or lower costs? The answer was all three, but without clarity, the technology was solving in circles. When consultants finally helped uncover that existing sensor data could predict many failures if integrated with maintenance schedules, the path forward became clearer. The lesson was painful but important: discovery must precede deployment.

These stories reflect a broader truth: transformation succeeds when organizations define process before selecting platforms. Internal teams can surface the pain points. Consultants can sharpen the framing and add an outside perspective. Vendors can demonstrate what is technically feasible. But the sequence matters. Process leads; platform follows.

Leaders often ask me: How long will it take, and how much will it cost? The honest answer is that it depends less on the tool and more on the discipline of preparation. Discovery may take weeks, prototyping may take months, and scaling may take more than a year. Costs are not just licenses and compute power; they also include the time invested by subject matter experts, the integration effort with legacy systems, and the governance structures needed to sustain trust. Organizations that rush past these steps almost always pay more later in rework and misalignment.

The best leaders also know when to stop. Not every AI initiative should move forward. The right question is not "can the tool do it" but "is this aligned to a strategic priority, do we have the data to support it, do we have the talent to oversee it, and can we measure impact in the next year?" If those answers are shaky, it is wiser to pause or defer than to proceed for the sake of appearances.

This discipline may sound like it slows things down, but in reality, it is what accelerates true progress. When the process is clear, platforms can be selected with precision, employees can adopt them with confidence, and customers can experience improvements that are real rather than cosmetic.

I often compared it to my own approach whenever I was handed a new program. The instinct could have been to jump into execution, but my first step was almost always to ask for financials by product, service, and market. I wanted to see where the business was actually done, which customers mattered most, and where the impact of change would be felt. Sharing that story with the team gave us a common language, grounding our work not in abstract tools but in real outcomes.

The companies that thrive in the AI era will not be those that chase platforms the fastest. They will be those who practice dual discovery, clarifying the business problem while staying open to what new technology can enable. They will resist the temptation to confuse speed with progress and instead build the discipline to align the process with purpose before selecting a platform.

When that happens, AI becomes more than a tool. It becomes an accelerator of solutions that were already well defined, grounded in the clarity of process, and aligned with the wisdom of people.

BRIDGE FROM PART 3 TO PART 4 – PREPARING FOR WHAT COMES NEXT

Up to this point, we've focused on the present: breaking down silos, evaluating breakdowns, assembling teams, and applying intelligence wisely. But transformation is not only about today's challenges. It is about preparing for tomorrow.

The leaders of the next era will need more than technical fluency. They will need curiosity, resilience, and the ability to guide people through uncertainty. They will have to balance data with judgment, and AI with purpose. And investors will seek out organizations that treat intelligence as a strategic asset, not a passing fad.

Part 4 looks forward to the skills, mindsets, and investments that will shape the future of intelligent organizations.

PART 4

Future-Focused Leadership

CHAPTER 11

PREPARING THE NEXT-GEN WORKFORCE

Data has always been at the center of our lives. What has changed is the recognition of its transformative power in shaping the information age. Looking ahead, the leaders who thrive will not simply be those who can use AI tools, but rather those who understand how data is created, connected, and turned into intelligence. Technology may set the foundation, but it is people, their judgment, curiosity, and wisdom who unlock the gains on that investment.

Some might argue that critical thinking has always been a leadership priority, and they would be right. What is different today is the context. In the past, critical thinking meant evaluating reports, weighing trade-offs, or questioning assumptions based on human-prepared data. With the rise of AI, information now arrives instantly, appears authoritative, and often looks more convincing than it really is. This is where the danger lies. Large language models generate text that sounds correct but may not be accurate. Algorithms inherit the limitations of their training data. And the speed at which AI accelerates decision-making can pressure leaders into acting quickly rather than wisely. Leaders must learn to look past surface fluency, slow down enough to verify, and ask the harder questions: Where did this data come from? Whose perspective is missing? What are the risks of acting on it as-is?

Critical thinking in the AI era is no longer optional. It has become the first line of defense against overconfidence in machine outputs and the key to using data responsibly.

Equally vital is emotional intelligence. Of all the skills that will define future leaders, it may be the most underestimated, often dismissed as a "soft skill" when in reality it is the hardest to master. AI can process patterns at scale, but it cannot read the room. It cannot sense hesitation in someone's voice during a meeting or the unspoken fears of a team facing new technology. Emotional intelligence is what connects data to people, translating insights into actions that others trust and follow.

In my own career, I have seen this play out again and again. The most pivotal moments weren't always about the dashboards or financial models. They came in conversations with employees who worried that a new system would add work, or worse, make their role obsolete. Listening carefully revealed that what looked like resistance was often fear of being left behind. What mattered most wasn't more data; it was empathy, reassurance, and clarity. That is emotional intelligence in practice.

Stay Hungry, Stay Curious

The next generation of leaders will need emotional intelligence not only to calm fears but to inspire curiosity. It transforms feedback into growth and setbacks into resilience. It helps leaders bridge silos by allowing them to understand the motivations of people outside their own function. In a global, AI-driven world, emotional intelligence will no longer be optional. It will be a competitive differentiator, the ability to lead with both head and heart.

If emotional intelligence is the foundation, then curiosity is the spark. The leaders of tomorrow will be defined by their willingness to ask better questions, to test assumptions, and to search for what might be missing. Adaptability will be equally important. In fast-moving environments, leaders must be comfortable with experimentation, iteration, and learning quickly from both successes and setbacks. And while data will always play a central role, the ability to tell its story is what transforms numbers into action. Storytelling with data is not about dumbing down complexity. It is about shaping insights in ways that resonate, build trust, and influence decisions across functions and audiences.

Climb Lattices, Not Ladders

For decades, the dominant career model was linear: climbing the ladder step by step toward greater responsibility. In the age of AI, that model is shifting. The leaders most in demand will not necessarily be those who moved upward fastest, but those who broadened their perspectives by moving across functions, industries, and disciplines. I learned this lesson in my own path. Stepping from accounting into supply chain, from product to service transformation, and from regulatory compliance to digital reinvention—each move gave me a wider view of how organizations work and where they break down. The next generation of leaders must seek out these same opportunities, not as detours but as vital steps in building the empathy, perspective, and systems-level thinking that AI-enabled organizations require.

Business schools are evolving from case studies of the past to simulations of the future, embedding data literacy, systems thinking, and ethics into their curricula. But it is not only technical knowledge that matters. Liberal arts programs are producing communicators, ethicists, and historians who remind us that technology has context. Engineers and scientists are learning to design with human impact in mind. Clinicians are being trained to balance medical expertise with digital literacy so that technology enhances, rather than replaces, care. Professional development within organizations must shift as well. The most effective companies will not attempt to turn every employee into a data scientist. Instead, they will create "data academies" that teach employees across roles how to ask better questions, how to use AI responsibly, and how to work alongside technical experts.

Purpose is the New Profit

Perhaps the most important mindset shift for the next generation is mission-driven leadership. Data and AI must be viewed not only as tools for profit but as levers for solving broader challenges. Whether addressing inequities in healthcare, building more sustainable supply chains, or tackling climate change, the leaders of tomorrow will be measured not just by shareholder returns but by the ecosystems they help build and the positive impact they deliver. This is not idealism. It is strategy. Organizations that cultivate leaders who balance profit with purpose will attract stronger talent, earn deeper trust, and ultimately endure longer than those who view data only through a narrow, financial lens.

Preparing the next generation workforce is not the job of business schools alone. It is a shared responsibility across disciplines, industries, and organizations. What unites all these efforts is the need to produce leaders who treat data as intelligence—human, contextual, emotional, and mission-driven. The leaders who thrive will be those who combine critical thinking with emotional intelligence, curiosity with adaptability, and technical fluency with ethical judgment. They will be the ones who see beyond dashboards to people, who use AI not as a crutch but as a catalyst, and who measure their success not only in profits, but in progress.

CHAPTER 12

INVESTING IN INTELLIGENT ORGANIZATIONS

Investors, boards, and stakeholders today ask a deceptively simple question: how do we identify which organizations are truly ready for the age of AI? The answer is not in who can boast the shiniest platform or the largest model, but in who uses data as intelligence, which is human, contextual, and strategically aligned.

Over the years, whenever I began a new program, one of my first requests was to see the financials: the products and services sold by market, the margins, and the customer mix. Numbers alone rarely told the whole story, but they revealed where the business was done globally and where customer behavior shaped results. Sharing those insights with teams helped tell the story of impact. It grounded our decisions, not in hype, but in facts that reflected both opportunity and risk.

That same lens applies to investing. The question isn't just who is adopting AI, but who is integrating it wisely, where the numbers, processes, and human decisions align.

The Creators, Users, and Builders

Some companies are creators, inventing the chips, algorithms, and models that power the infrastructure of AI. They are high-risk and high-reward, depending on breakthroughs and defensibility. Others are users who embed AI into retail, manufacturing, finance, or healthcare. These companies may look ordinary, but their strength lies in treating intelligence as a strategic asset, streamlining product portfolios, reducing friction in customer experience, or strengthening resilience through smarter operations. And then there are the ecosystem builders: firms that don't just optimize their own performance but connect players across industries. They thrive in the spaces between, orchestrating data so that suppliers, partners, governments, and even competitors can solve shared challenges together.

I've seen glimpses of this orchestration in action. When working on compliance initiatives that began in one region but cascaded globally, it became clear how interconnected the system really was. A single regulatory shift could ripple across supply chains, product portfolios, and customer communications. The companies that navigated best were those that aligned cross-functionally, treated intelligence as shared, and built trust with partners rather than working in isolation. For investors, that kind of collaboration is a leading signal of maturity.

Of course, not every claim of "AI transformation" should be taken at face value. There are companies layering buzzwords onto their pitch decks without tying results to measurable outcomes. Some spend heavily on platforms without clarity of process. Others lean too hard on automation and strip away human oversight, putting trust and brand reputation at risk. These are the red flags. They remind us that intelligence is not about tools alone, but about discipline, governance, and context.

The opportunity ahead spans every sector. In healthcare, the strongest signals are platforms that connect providers, payers, and patients to improve outcomes and reduce disparities. In finance, firms use AI for fraud detection and risk modeling with transparency and oversight. In manufacturing, predictive maintenance keeps plants running while improving safety. In retail and marketplaces, it is recommendation engines and logistics platforms that build ecosystems where millions of participants can operate with trust.

The organizations that will define the next wave will not only use AI to compete; they will use it to convene. They will integrate data across industries, create hybrids of automation and expertise, and build sustainability platforms that align economic and social goals. These are the firms investors should look for, the ones creating value not only within their walls, but across networks that shape entire markets.

The real test of an intelligent organization is not whether it has AI, but whether it has clarity: clear strategy, connected data, a workforce prepared to collaborate with machines, and leaders who model curiosity, adaptability, and ethics. For investors, boards, and stakeholders, those are the signals to watch.

The AI era will certainly create winners and losers. The winners will be those who balance efficiency with responsibility, competition with collaboration, and technology with human judgment. They will outperform not simply because they are fast, but because they are wise.

That wisdom is what makes intelligence truly strategic. It is what transforms data into decisions, platforms into ecosystems, and opportunities into outcomes that endure.

CONCLUSION

BIGGER, BETTER FUTURE

If you've made it here, thank you. Thank you for your time, your focus, and your willingness to look past the shiny tools to the harder, more human work underneath. The big idea of this book is simple: AI isn't enough. Intelligence comes from how people use data, connect processes, and make decisions together. The rest is just speed.

What I have learned across my career, whether working in accounting, supply chain, product transformations, or customer experience, is that breakthroughs rarely come from perfect plans. They come from curiosity. They come from the courage to ask, "Is there a better way?" They come from listening to the people closest to the work, and from finding allies in unexpected places. Those experiences gave me perspective and resilience, but more importantly, they revealed the extraordinary capacity of teams who build together.

That is the rally call I want to leave you with. Seek out those same opportunities. For employees, it means saying yes to projects that stretch you, that force you to see beyond your lane. For leaders, it means creating the conditions where your teams feel safe to ask hard questions and to experiment with better answers. For investors and boards, it means rewarding the organizations that treat intelligence not as hype, but as a strategic asset: human, contextual, and mission-driven.

So what now? Start small. Walk the floor with your teams or take a figurative lap through your processes. Ask the obvious questions. Look for the places where handoffs wobble, where context goes missing, where people feel unheard. Treat data like a shared language. Finance, operations, product, and service all need a voice. Put process before platform. **If you cannot explain the "what" and "why" in a paragraph, you are not ready for the "with which tool."** And above all, keep humans in the loop. Let AI scale patterns, but let people set purpose.

Because that is what transformation really is. It is not about dramatic leaps. It is about steady, intentional steps forward. The next good decision. The next connection made. The next small win that grows into something larger when a team, an organization, or even an ecosystem pulls together.

AI isn't enough. But you—your leadership, your investments, your judgment, your willingness to connect the dots—just might be. That is the bigger, better future: one built on human wisdom, strengthened by AI, and driven by the courage to act.

The work starts now. And it starts with you.

FINAL THOUGHTS

When I set out to write this book, I wasn't trying to add another voice to the AI noise. I wanted to capture the lessons that come from lived experience, from the messy meetings, the late-night problem-solving, and the moments when a team finally cracks the code on something that's been stuck for too long.

If there's one thing I hope you carry with you, it's that transformation is not abstract. It's not happening "out there" in some distant future. It happens right where you are—in the conversations you lead, the questions you ask, the risks you take, and the people you choose to listen to.

I've walked into projects with no script, no perfect playbook, and plenty of skepticism in the room. What made the difference was curiosity, humility, and the willingness to build trust across silos. That's the work of leadership. It's also the work of humanity.

So as you close this book, don't think of it as an ending. Think of it as an invitation. Look at your organization, your industry, your community, and ask yourself what part you can play in creating something bigger and better.

AI will be there, as a tool and a partner. But the real future will be written by people who have the courage to act with wisdom, context, and purpose. My hope is that you're one of them.

ABOUT THE AUTHOR

Jane DiMartino is a transformation leader, strategist, and consultant with more than 20 years of experience helping organizations in healthcare, medtech, financial services, and consumer goods connect data, people, and processes. Through JBM Consulting, she partners with companies to drive operational excellence, digital transformation, and AI-enabled innovation. Her work has spanned global compliance programs, product-to-service transformations, and customer experience redesigns, always grounded in the belief that human judgment and collaboration are what make data intelligent.

Jane is also passionate about mentoring the next generation of leaders, weaving together curiosity, emotional intelligence, and mission-driven purpose.

Contact
Readers, leaders, and organizations interested in continuing the conversation can connect with Jane here:

- Website: https://jbmaiconsulting.squarespace.com/
- LinkedIn: www.linkedin.com/in/janedimartino

www.ingramcontent.com/pod-product-compliance
Lightning Source LLC
Chambersburg PA
CBHW050513210326
41521CB00011B/2442